# BUILD YOURSELF A BOAT

## *The BreakBeat Poets* Series

### ABOUT THE BREAKBEAT POETS SERIES

The BreakBeat Poets series, curated by Kevin Coval and Nate Marshall, is committed to work that brings the aesthetic of hip-hop practice to the page. These books are a cipher for the fresh, with an eye always to the next. We strive to center and showcase some of the most exciting voices in literature, art, and culture.

### BREAKBEAT POETS SERIES TITLES INCLUDE:

*The BreakBeat Poets: New American Poetry in the Age of Hip-Hop*, edited by Kevin Coval, Quraysh Ali Lansana, and Nate Marshall

*This is Modern Art: A Play*, Idris Goodwin and Kevin Coval

*The BreakBeat Poets Vol 2: Black Girl Magic*, edited by Mahogany L. Browne, Jamila Woods, and Idrissa Simmonds

*Human Highlight*, Idris Goodwin and Kevin Coval

*On My Way to Liberation*, H. Melt

*Black Queer Hoe*, Britteney Black Rose Kapri

*Citizen Illegal*, José Olivarez

*Graphite*, Patricia Frazier

*The BreakBeat Poets Vol 3: Halal If You Hear Me*, edited by Fatimah Asghar and Safia Elhillo

*Commando*, E'mon Lauren

# BUILD YOURSELF A BOAT

*Camonghne Felix*

Haymarket Books
Chicago, Illinois

Published in 2019 by
Haymarket Books
P.O. Box 180165
Chicago, IL 60618
www.haymarketbooks.org

ISBN: 978-1-60846-611-5

Distributed to the trade in the US through Consortium Book Sales and
Distribution (www.cbsd.com) and internationally through Ingram Publisher
Services International (www.ingramcontent.com).

This book was published with the generous support of Lannan Foundation
and Wallace Action Fund.

Cover design by Brett Neimann.

Printed in Canada by union labor.

10 9 8 7 6 5 4 3 2

# CONTENTS

*"I'm goin' look for my body, yeah—I'll be back like real soon…"*

Solange Knowles

*"If ruin was my sole inheritance, and the only certainty the impossibility of recovering the stories of the enslaved, did this make my history tantamount to mourning? Or worse, was it a melancholia I would never be able to overcome?"*

Saidiya Hartman, *Lose Your Mother*

# LOST POEM 4: RX

The psych on duty in triage
Asks me if I want to die, and I say

Not at the moment, no, but stay
Tuned. I can charm my way out

Of anything—including his seven-day
Suggested stay, those ugly

Gray mornings buzzing in infrasound
I can save my own life just as easily

As I can corrupt compounds of
Ripe silence with just a mouth—

Drown it out of its own sound.
This is what makes me dangerously

Compatible with death
Me and my ability to finesse

Choice out of desire, the talented
Tenth of disassociation, the power

Of being just a body within a body
Of jewels.

# CONTOURING THE FLATTENING

I try not to tell about the stories
still bleeding. After all, who wishes
to lead their own mother to wolves.

I try not to mess with the shape of
my privilege. I only say what they
need to hear. If the they is an us
I make myself an example. I lie to
keep it all intact.

But if I felt I could, I would unstitch
this plaque sewn over my
mouth. I would tell you of the seasonal

allergies, how my primary doctor warned
my mother of dead cockroaches, their
eggs, the likelihood of them in my lungs.

I would tell of how often we'd bomb the house,
how I'd spend summer nights collecting little brown
skeletons in the thousands, every inhale ending
in a question of poison.

I would tell of the mice that sometimes bit
us in our sleep, how the infestation of them
violated any concept of domain—how
we could not know who the house really
belonged to; a house of rodents, or of men

but I keep my sob stories to myself[1]. I keep my
smile white and my fists closed. I let survival be
survival. I grow into the shoe. I keep the world
big and my sanity small.

---

# CUTTING W/ JB

JB's getting her ass bussed in the other room. We can hear the clap-clap of wet flesh over the whip of the ceiling fan above. The heat in the projects is always on and thick and coming for your edges except for the days when you really need it, when it's five degrees with wind chill and Housing won't come fix your broken bedroom window. It's half past midday and by now I'm bored enough to maybe consider going back to school but they won't let me in this late in the day anyway, so I have to sit with the decision I've made. No one's looking for us. Emmy's mom died five weeks ago, so as far as she's concerned, what the fuck is a parent? I've never had a best friend before. All the books say that when your best friend's mama die, you ain't got no parents neither. We spend our days in patient wanderlust, living off sheer probability in a series of cheap, rancid thrills.

# IMAGINE??? MY SISTER AN ASTRONAUT???

When she was small I couldn't see
her I held her hand in tendered

obligation fed her because
she was hungry

slapped her because
she spoke one day she stole

my underwear
I climbed to the top of

our bunk beds my waist a cradle over her's
my fists a marsh of dead moons

shadowing her little face
after two taps I felt the

monstrosity of my putrid desires
flatten

my intrinsic knowings
suddenly afraid to bruise the small

genius
the strange foreign god of sisterhood

it was then I knew
I loved her something bad

she's off to college going to study
some aerospace biomedical nanoscience

shit some shit only white people think
to study because access is a frame

of reference an organizing principle
in the family group chat she sweats us out

with her excitement about next semester
and 8 a.m. trig

in high school I failed everything
graduated with underwhelming decimals

the dark trauma of men lining my transcript
but baby girl has got something

I don't
it's called discipline and

it moves her through the world slow
and deliberate all the night a platform

all the trains just stations away
she's off to space camp in a few weeks

and so fucking casual about it I say, hey
maybe you should be an astronaut yea, thinking

about it as if it were a breakfast burrito or
mommy's oxtail

my girl my young knight
driving a needle through the inflated

boundaries of ambiguous sciences I think
shiiiiiiit imagine?? My sister an astronaut???

lineage narrated through the brat
of my heart into

the prodigious stuff of the stars
towering in bigness

bigger than you and you and you
and you and you.

## GOOGLE SEARCH KEYWORDS:

blood; in; underwear

kids; having; sex

cousin; love

incest; what; is

what; is; molest

what; is; rape

how; to; know

rape;

cousin; loves; cousin

incest; what; is

how; to; die; on; purpose

how; to; tie; noose

how; to; starve

8

how; many; Tylenol

Thirty; Tylenol?

Seventy-Five; Tylenol?

how; to; get; blood; out

kid; raping; kid[2]

---

# THINGS THE BLOCK TAUGHT ME

Lesson 1:

Finish The Job.

When Tasha died, we figured that she had been
zippered open
neck first
like a spayed swan.

I am fourteen. I am only as large as my fists. I am being
introduced to the bold swagger of knuckle to bone.
It's a drug. A girl curls under the drag of my left hook.
I am only as large as my fists. I am a giant

extinguishing a bulb.

# WHITE HOUSE

Maybe I should have waited,
given my body more time


let the pearling of that new
Moon really settle in, burrow in
its call to me, but I had shit to do
and me to do and I forget
the gall of the political—
how it begs against the centering
of self, begs you to meet
your wrangled drama at the
door. I will always have
the trouble of
my need to do what I'm told
and my need to do
what I'm led to. I didn't worry
that it was too late, I didn't
worry about him at all—my body
a salt capsule to drown, little concern
for my pilot.

All I can do now is swim good
good love, take note of the golds that
work me down, the shifts that calm my cool. I'm
taking it East, steady on my slow
walk to the capital of my councils,
steady on the way to forgiving my fissures, counting
my crows. God knows I'm a creature
of mystic, God knows I'm a creature of critical
holes, I was given a life and led
it off and astray toward the glitter of

11

direction. I know now what
thickened the breath, what blackened the
wound.

In the mirror I count the
new grids, the crimson lines of
life's torture coloring
the sugar of my thighs.

In addiction, the stakes are alive.

In illness, the stakes—they hide,
they sputter, they die.

## STATEMENT FROM CAMONGHNE FELIX ON THE MURDERS OF JESSE WASHINGTON, STEPHON CLARK AND HER ATTEMPT TO UNDERSTAND THE PSYCHOLOGY OF LYNCHING:

**For Immediate Release:**

**Brooklyn, NY**—I try to imagine myself threading a small mouse on a spit the same mouse that we found hampering in my pink bed sheets as I attempt a petrified sleep a textured sleep one salted with the humiliation of poverty I try to imagine myself in the midst of that sleep quilted addled in it unable to restrain the tiny evils inside of me but I can't get past the first pinch of gelled flesh I can't get past the trauma of puncturing a thing that bleeds blood no matter how it beetles through my night no matter how it shames me out of my interior cultures I can't get past its squeals I can't get past the inhumanity I can't get past the lie but the gods of small things become the god of all things in the dark

###

# THANK GOD I CAN'T DRIVE

My brain is trying so hard to outrun this.
It is doing more work than the lie.

I could go to jail for anything. I look like that
kind of girl. I only speak one language. I am

of prestige but can't really prove it. Not if
my hands are tied. Not if my smartphone is

seized. Not if you can't google me. Without
an archive of human bragging rights, I'm

fucking nobody, an empty bag, two-toned
luggage. I'm not trying to be sanctimonious,

I just found out that I'm afraid to die, like,
there goes years of posturing about, beating it

like I own it, taking it to the bathroom with
the tampons—like, look at me, I am so agent

and with all this agency I can just deploy
death at any time. The truth is

that I'm already on the clock, I'm just a few
notches down on the "black-girl-with-bad

mouth" list, the street lights go out and I'm
just at the mercy of my own bravery and

their punts of powerlessness, their "who
the hell do you think you are's?"

# ZIMMERMAN TESTIMONIES: DAY 1

*These assholes, they always get away*
—George Zimmerman

And then the sky is bleeding
a soft cry, and I am at the head
of it; a six-pane window, a vein of
lightning, a bath in immanence and
what kind of Arizona, which pack of
Skittles. I like the Darkside pack but those
came out last winter, Tray's body already a
dovetail in moist ground and which newscast
had his father come home to arrange the dry bones
in front of and how long had he waited for his one boy
to return from wherever night-crested boys roam in the salt
of Floridian south and who plans to rob anything in socks and
sandals, and in the courtroom the prosecutor taps play on the
tape, Trayvon's wet scream the only thing living a full life
and his mother, a mare overwrought with the front seat
of her son's slaughter, chases the breath out
of the courtroom, the big door whipping
behind her, running and running
every day of this trial he dies

And then
slides of his
body, head north,
limbs gutted,
a massy constellation,
the bubbling in his chest,
a county officer attempts to revive the breath
a plastic grocery bag, vaseline, the stuffing of the entrance
wound
"no sir," "not on my list of priorities, sir" "to preserve the
integrity
of the body, sir" it is how we mourn, the spectator
consumed with the positioning of slain skin
wherever I am in the world, my tattered arms the
fictive recital of an old girl born again and again into
breathlessness, and who
would I be, if not my blue-black self, if not my call to
the forest that columns in rings around me, if not the
affection
that brings me to loss and now the top of Zimmerman's
head, day of murder
smudges of foreign blood staggered through the scalp

# CUTTING W/ JB

We're play fighting in the hallway, bowling each other down three flights. We're bruised and tickled about the idiocy of it, the pain creeping up later on delayed limbs. "You gotta get tougher, Momo" Emmy says, launching a right hook into the elastic of my left jaw, displacing my sense of moment and knocking the time back. ACS says Emmy has to go live with her biological mom in Minnesota, who she's only ever known as Miss Mary. There's a lofty countdown precipitating, filling up the cavities. We've grown apt at repurposing our emotions. She's not leaving yet, and we keep discussing the forever of our best friendship, but the adults burgeoning in us both know the mirage of infinity. Somehow, we end up with the same bleeding gash, of the same shape, on the same arm. We're not sure how it's possible. Eventually it keloids—and memory[3] perforates the body.

3    *I always remembered the story, it's just that I thought I did not know*

# GOOGLE SEARCH KEYWORDS:

Having; strange; dreams

owls; crippled; bleeding

what; is; dreaming

do; owls; dream

what; is; drowning

what; non; human; forges; marks

who; is; eve

where's; eve's; child

in; what; garden

in; what; fold

                                        nativity; in; question

                    species; on; earth

species; in; question


                what; else; gives; birth



                            what; else; calls; war



what; else; builds; nest


                            what; else; summons; fire; to; feed

# CUTTING W/ JB

Emmy's fingers are fat and the beds chafed from the cheap ass lighters we've been lifting from Family Dollar. We've resolved that my spliffs pull the best because I've got my mother's piano hands and I'm the only one who can roll the J tight-tight, like a multihull anchored and drawn in, like it wasn't meant to hold a breath to begin with, even in this cold ass weather. JB wants Emmy and I to cut the rest of classes with her [entails a stealth escape after third period, a run through an unsupervised emergency exit, a three-way split to distract the twelve security guards who aren't looking at all] because she wants to go see about this dude she's been fucking with.[4] He says his mom is in Jamaica for a week [which makes his mama's living room the turn up trap] and JB's been stuck babysitting for the past few days and needs to be fucked right now, first period. She's older than all of us, a super super super senior—we assume that her seniority makes her the queen of sexual prowess and we want nothing more than to baste ourselves in all of her dirt.

---

4    *It's a little fuzzy, but I remember trying to grab the ladder and he kept*

# TRAP QUEEN

I'm your Trap Queen.

In these shorts, I'm all ass.
My clap don't quiet. My tongue don't lie.

In these shorts I'm just glitchy melanin,
wholly octagonal—did you know

I've got edges? Did you know I've got
corners? Can you call that anything but

dynamic? But a port with a flint?
Trap Queen so notorious

they don't even know what she look like.
Trap Queen so careless

she errybody's boo
errybody first love—take her to the mall

     she gon *buss it open 4 a ni\*\*a*
she errybody's thot, errybody good fuck.

Trap Queen so spectacular she everybody's tit.
Trap Queen is everybody's mama. Everybody's

abandoned land. Errybody excuse. She
errybody's lifelong lament, but turn the

floodlights off, and errybody motivated by
how nimble her knee, how she make you

come with just the way she put her black on.

You love that shit, the way
she flex in it, put her whole foot in it, so black

you can't divorce it, so black you don't speak
her language, black in your wet dream, she come

Black. Her black is residual
will not wash out of the duvet

And keep it real
you love that shit

love to deliver it, send the wet silencer
down her throat, love to shut her up but

      Trap Queen don't fear shit except how easily
      my body leaves me, how often it is not mine.

      Trap Queen don't fear shit, except an unlimited
      caricature, except the way they tow my narrative

      right out of my own mouth and iron it out flat.
      Trap Queen don't fear shit, except for how

      errybody lay claim when the sun falls, except
      for how I can't keep a moment of myself to

      myself. Don't fear shit except the way my
      lonesome is your invitation, the way

      all my power sustains and sanctifies,
      the way the world will lay

its violence at the threat
of my able black body.

Except the way nobody
got my back until I'm face forward

an obituary or
a red prayer orbiting until

errybody forget about it
& find my sister. & repeat.

# ON ENTROPY

*after Yasamin Ghiasi*

"There are more people alive now than there
are dead in the earth," an article says. I keep
telling myself to invest in entropy, or at least
in defining it. In contending with it. Decom-
position is a performance of exponential
dignity. An act of stripping what life-worn
fabrics perforate the borders between lyric
and magic. I want to step out of my language
and light up, but the body is a container.
The body is a mold; I fit snugly; I can barely
breathe in here. Leave me. I've got to count
the dead in here. I'm an atom, and I'm new
to the water. I got born by expanding. I get
born every day: my flesh is so damn raw with
all this entering.

# STATEMENT ON BEING LONELY VS. ALONE

**On Background:** I think carefully about assumptions on my
walk home     I hold the map of the moon at the base of my
neck balancing on   orbs   and    light    and  pride and shit
     heartbreak is     an oily    firewall    a permutation    I
fall    victim to my need to be small              even when    I
pull             the Sun. The Hierophant. The Ace of Cups.
  even with this vice of wealth in practice       grace in sheer
ability
I tell my girls     it's all good     cause'         I cross with    the
Two of Cups every time     I fill up         I am at capacity    I
sit
contradicted in my lonesomeness       in how much I rely on
consolation as validation    I know better than to vote     against
myself         cancel myself out in negatives         be kind
to my friend, Kayla says     and boy     am I trying       this
Newport     a foxtail    with its hand in its mouth    I shell out
to breathe better         I shrink to belong[5]

---

5    *He must have tried to hold me,*

# LOST POEM #5: I WON'T EVEN ASK WHY

I try not to think about
why all the black men
on Tinder signed up
for Tinder to date white
women

Instead I daydream myself
into frameless fantasies
with the bartender, Questlove's
drummer, the unattainable

currents of harmless
want, the impossible
4 a.m. solace of being
touched gingerly
in my sleep.

# OR, IT'S ALL IN MY HEAD

*"If this happens to you, what do you want me to do?"*

*"Burn the city down."*

The poem could just die right here
    but it is not at all tempered
    not any of it real
    I crawl into his lap, put my mouth
            to his cheek and scream, holler, you can still hear
                    me, can't you?

I am incredibly generous this night, I say we can
    watch anything you want my love
        is a mourning animal
            all I see is dead

men all I see is this
    rotten, bulbous nightmare
          looping, chasing your back down, clipping the
road in front I am only a warrior in my sleep,
      who will I be in the 28 hours that follow only the body
                can tell really.

## GOOGLE SEARCH KEYWORDS:

radio; disney

judy; Blume

hey; god; it's; me;

cognitive; behavioral; therapy

moby; dick

p; t; s; d

jesse; mccartney

how; to; know; if; boys; like; you

how; to; get; blood; out

how; to; know; if; girls; like; you

lesbians;

how; to; overdose

how; to; make; yourself; quiet; forever

mute;

# LESSON, UNMITIGATED

sometimes I am convinced                                    of my
luck
   might share it    sell it for soft french bread

   & a pool of Sauvignon    Instead I hear the call of
grand bravery,

my whole life some   God's staff   yo   the universe has
got this
   sick ability to fuck   all the gold away    literally
                        towing it
                        right out

   the mouth   elasticity a bone first   all bend a
lesson toward
later. I'm crying out from the wounding and

     surviving the lash.

# NO RELIEF

*For Tameka Norris*

1.  Blood maps the artifice of
    the fictional state. The forward
    body is a fictional state. The body
    happens on the line. The forward
    body is a state between what
    eludes and what propels the
    circulation of "No."

2.  They are so enamored with
    witnessing excretion. Here.
    Here's your fucking art. The
    stroke consistent and spitting
    and jiving the berry from the
    branch.

3.  Wishing the hoof alive. Putting my
    foot in the wall. Selling the scream
    to buy back the seam. The forward
    body becoming artifice, propelling
    some seamed circulation/regulation
    of "No."

4.  The marginal system.

5.  Where she could paint but chooses to bleed instead.

# DISCLAIMER

This is not an attempt at confessional poetry, nor is it a gesture toward postmodernist conceptual lit. The body is not a site for revelatory shame. Assembly of self is not voyeuristic. All publicly recognizable characters, settings, and names cited in this collection are the property of themselves. & no copyright infringement was intended.

# MIRROR TALK

am I allowed to disrespect the form. am I allowed to instead proclaim that he just raped me. that it just happened. that he just did. that I was small and formidable, a fruit or something else taking in from a sun and expanding. am I allowed to say that I didn't write it for you. am I allowed to say that I've fucked four women and three men and still liked it, even though. am I allowed to say that I didn't do it for him or because of the other him him, or to heal, or to mitigate[6] the gods' monopoly on wellness—but to be an organ in post survival, a dim sound existing retroactively, a full circle sold.

---

6    *it's just that I thought I did not know how to swim and it dawned on me that*
     *not only did I know,*

# POLICE

law is body talk. law arches the forked road/ the breadth of any choice stretches and collects volume/ *I've never met anyone like you before*/ law functions in height when the lights go off/ the lights are off/ where are his hands?/ the law towers and flickers, at most/ but did it lie?/ why are the lights off?/ law is man/ the law abandons language in the dark/ the law sequesters the cool of the silence/ he presses his forearm across my back like a live rod/ like law/ *don't act like you don't want to*[7]/I quell the breath of it to occupy the sound/ the law prefers disease/ my word pales cocktail pink against his.

7   *They kept apologizing to me and he was twitchin'*

# GROCERY

I'm trying to get it all
Out and it burns like

Fucking hell, and I'm
So pissed off and all

There is to me is what
Silence I can't conquer

I'm guilty of throwing
Drinks at it, keying its

Car, saying fuck you
Here's my ass to kiss

Here's my tongue to
Split, my body to butterfly

I don't have any mother
Fucking poems, I can't

Write because it doesn't
Really count, does it

The time I spend chasing
The cat that got out, the

Time it spends trying to
Get back to the shelter

Man made in ignorance.
Maybe I am not meant

For your nature, maybe I'm
A humble, sprawling beast

Maybe I eat up the produce
Before it ripes, maybe that's

All that matters in loving any-
Thing, that it has time to

Brown before the hunger
Covets the starch.

# SLEEPING ON ADDERALL

Here's a board and a bold move and a siphon of power and I'm not sleeping but I am overwhelmed with my own stiff bones with the rigidity of being strong always handling always beyond my years def dying faster than everyone else.

Here's a reason to wear some white kind of dance with it be the yolk of things and float and here's strong again, the irrevocable contract, here's what comes with all the cool yellow scaffolding my mornings here's the rain and I can either dance in it or walk like everyone else it's the thread veined right through me perspective only a shared tool.

It's fine I've got to stop writing love poems anyway it's not conducive to the project stick to the project there are oceans and oceans and I am just one querulous petulant fish glittering and considering the upstream[8].

8    *In any event, I digress.*

# ZIMMERMAN TESTIMONIES: DAY 4

then 24 hours later and
Rachel is still on the stand
you can see the arid contempt in the glass
eye of the prosecutor, the steel disregard
for grief, the swiveled shoulder affect

                          I'm thinking about third grade.
                 I'm thinking about the time they told me
                     not to lie and I didn't but they said
     I did and I'm thinking about how slowly their mouths
         shape at me before I'm angry enough to chat back
   and I'm thinking about the vertical perk in the eyebrow
                                when
           I chew a word they don't expect and how
         the narrative goes from miss to Ma'am once
           you've mastered the Master's language
     and I'm thinking about it and thinking about it
                  "you speak so well"

and thinking about what if I didn't.

# TONYA HARDING'S FUR COATS

The thing about being poor      is that you spend your days
pointing

    in quiet humor

        noting every motherless origin
        every gap     in the moral fortitude
        of the wealthy

you know     a coat

    is never just     a coat

but dead &       fresh
animals     stripped    & bled

   all    affirmations of our curational pieties

our inhumanities bold and bighearted       by the casual

        pleasures of warmth

It's in the kill that we see

    how   poverty precludes   the   conceit of envy.

     In the fog of my first tunneled spiral

      I saw the drug of that magic

      that blade in the shoulder of grace

That cold floor a gallery of small stars
     I learned the artifice of

          Falling

and gravity is
               but a single tiny hand

               of compulsive insignificance


                         There I was, welled in tar and fat and

     Committed to this   violently brave

          Sport, a girl unusual and generously unashamed

     My face still freckled with the glee

               of bare stripped winters          me and my ego
pretending

bringing us down into a two-footed spill

Demeter and her crops in rot

     What even am I except a perpetual resident

Of cold endings

          The knee snaps and that          was that


                              *"But, did you do it?*

                              *Are you sorry?"*

---------------------------------

*"But, did you do it?*

*Are you sorry?"*

　　　The knee snaps and that　　　was that

　　Of cold endings

　　　What even am I except a perpetual resident

Demeter and her crops in rot

bringing us down into a two-footed spill

　　　of bare stripped winters me and my ego pretending

　　My face still freckled with the glee

　　　　　Sport, a girl unusual and generously unashamed

　　Committed to this　　violently brave

　　　　　There I was, welled in tar and fat and

　　　　of compulsive insignificance

　　　but a single tiny hand

　and gravity is

　　　　Falling

　I learned the artifice of

That cold floor

That galley of small stars

That blade in the shoulder of grace

I saw the drug of the magic

In the fog of my first tunneled spiral

How          poverty precludes     the      conceit of envy.

It's in the kill that we see

pleasures of warmth

our inhumanities bold and bighearted     by the casual

all      affirmations of our curational pieties

Animals          stripped          & bled
but      dead &          fresh

is never just a coat

you know          a coat

of the wealthy
every gap          in the moral fortitude

noting every motherless origin

in quiet humor

The thing about being poor          is that you spend your days
pointing

# NO SHADE, THOUGH

a faculty member thinks I am too involved
in my own nostalgia. I say what nostalgia.

you mean black nostalgia. If I can't recall
the land of my umbilical severance then there

was no navel to begin with.
when the memory finds the self—tapered and

running out of space, it goes around asking
for its name and praying for the yes of a right answer.

that's not nostalgia. That's a requiem.
you assume that the source material

of a collective bleed could only be a misunderstanding
of placement. What do you mean?

I know where I am. These are the Americas. It is
2014. I know my name and why I'm not dead.

that is more than you can say for you. Knowing is
superior. Is infinite. To think nostalgic is to want for

something more beautiful than what sits dead
at your table. What we'd share tomorrow has starved

overnight. What we'd share tomorrow has already
left its stink in the bed.

## "BUT IN WHAT WAY DOES THE BLENDING OF TWO SLIGHTLY DIFFERENT CELLS BRING ABOUT SUCH A RENEWAL OF LIFE?" —FREUD

She bled out through the bone, once
bred childless, & I am the one that took final hold, made
    the novelty a rest stop—she doesn't
blame me, not now, now I'm a raft unswept in seizure
    Had I drowned though, had I
burned the flag, the grieving would have fluxed all
    breath, would have been homicide
Infection a lone province, illness merging at the center
    I've got no analogies for this reel[9],
only troubled gourds nourishing the crops—
    she made me with a thrill that stands
up, discs stacking over each other like whole moons
    "Don't give me any grandchildren,"
she says, "Not too soon." Because what a way to do
    faith, all the cells roused eternally
over the conspiracy of some other sovereign body

9    *How is it that I'm sane? Am I really sane? Okay, time to stop.*

# CUTTING W/ JB

We're consumed with this countdown now. Every day is a precursor to absence. Emmy's leaving, and I'm stuck. Things have been bad at home, and I've discovered a general hate for myself. It's after eleven, and I'm not allowed to talk on the phone at this hour, but I'm at a perpetual standoff with anything that compromises my authority over my own authority. I call Emmy from the bathtub. "How long have you been in the bathroom?" She asks, "Ages," I whisper, "I'm waiting for my mom to fall asleep." My mother says that the moment she sees a new cut on my arm she'll have me admitted again, immediately. I've gotten pretty good at disguising them as old wounds, but I need at least 8 hours of uninterrupted hiding to get away with it. The clawfoot bathtub allows for reclining. It'll do. I make it do. "Did you cut, Momo?" I let silence do the work. "Seriously Momo, what the fuck, are you going to kill yourself? My mom just died!" "I'm not going to kill myself." "Really," she asks, "because you've been cutting yourself like a fish every day, and I can't tell what's next." A breath. "Fine, Momo, you want more blood?" The phone drops, and I can hear footsteps on the other end. It's reclaimed, and her voice reappears. "Right now, there's a razor in my hand. I am going to cut myself with this razor every time you cut yourself, since you want to bleed so bad." I sigh, "is it the kind of razor you shave your legs with?" "Yes," she says. "Then you might want to come over here and get this box-cutter, because those razors not gon' cut."

AFTER THE ABORTION, AN OLDER WHITE PLANNED PARENTHOOD VOLUNTEER ASKS IF MY HUSBAND IS HERE & SQUEEZES MY THIGH AND SAYS, "YOU MADE THE RIGHT DECISION," AND THEN "LOOK WHAT COULD HAPPEN IF TRUMP WERE PRESIDENT, I MEAN, YOU MIGHT NOT EVEN BE HERE."

What else could    I say    except I    agree with you    really am bulldozed with grief
    my strength a whistle in this cold parabola    everything an arc nemesis    all of my self a bowl
    Instead I said    yes    he is here I mean my fiancé    I know    I made    the right decision    of
course he is okay    we already    agreed on this plan    I say I know    Look    I mean look what could    happen    she
says Hillary is our only option    I say I know    Look    I haven't told anyone this    I am quitting my job
she says    my god    I think I    understand your    geography no    not really    I mean I'm
leaving my good god government job    I work for    the    governor    she says are you running
I say    sort of I mean    I'm    going to work    for Hillary    for    America    because    we're
looking at a critical    fault    otherwise
    they need

    my colloquial    criticalities my    totalizing    abnormalities my    compounds and constructs of trajectory
this is the only how I know to be had    I belong to the    people but not your    people I mean
    I'm saying    my people    you wouldn't understand this    I'm stealthy and svelte    I can

counter-swell        any tide        I        am        prepared        she holds my hands        says thank
you        you must know that it        matters        all of it        matters
in the bed next to me a        woman solid with        anguish and sleep        is ruby with the wash of
bleeding out and        no one is        tending        I look down at myself, curried
with the same deep pink        realize no one is        tending in the taxi cab        my husband I mean fiancé
holds my hands his fingers        all lead        a dying creek at the pitch of        a sword        he says I'm okay
when        you're okay        you have to be okay        remember they're waiting        on you        for days I slept like this
my open submission        to the cosmic opacities        of time        my body shedding its just-
built        mouth        he lies awake        meters between        us
steady        documenting a        decay        my black studies professor said        what are you
here for        if        you're not        willing        to die for it        I        Get        It        I'm
skunked with        the fear of        what I'm willing        to kill for it        where do I file this nuance        to
whom do I spare this        complaint

When I woke        he'd been fed        watered        wanted for        realized he
didn't need my indecision        or        his inability to travel        time        or        the        bottomless
glamour of conquering the unknown        I know now the        octane        faults of our
ontological        duties        the war between becoming and        the formal        unbecoming of being
called and they said they        needed me        they did so I went        we bellied the hole        I did what
my mother        asked of me        stepped into the heavy        quilt of her        ill-drawn life        I did        my

fucking    job I did    what I was told  in the end all my chemistry a performance of gratitude    all
my insides turned    purple    with storms    on election
night I flipped from
channel to channel    neurosis in practice    as    weighted predictions balance
the draw I think    no oh please    don't
you know what I've bled    for this  in the distance a lone    voice is soprano with cheer and the silence
settles in    succeeds with    bare platitudes
I swear my love    I did my best I  worked with    what I know I tilled    I paved I
foraged labored  a land

got us   some    growth settled    my currents[1]    left    all of us

famished    bloody    hungry at    war.

10   *and somehow, as I don't remember, I got out the pool.*

The children
go out and reupholster
the day, strip themselves of asylum.
It's expensive and costs us a fever. It's
a matter of economic autonomy and I get the
selfishness of it; age suckles the bone and deploys a decay.
When I was a child, there were no lights. When I was a child
I burrowed in inflexible flesh. Give me your excuse and we'll
trade.

## BEER PONG

I'm a mess tonight. I'm unleavened and bellying in mercy. I get
high, then I'm a hearty catch. You can't un-see me, you're already
sewn in, I'm already a stiff hazard, you already want to be a
subject drowning. Ok, one more until a light goes out. Ok,
one more until this song stops corroding. You're
a one-stop shop and I'm an Atlantic
embargo. No, I'm keeping
this one as memento.
I get to collect
what I win.

# ZIMMERMAN TESTIMONIES: DAY 5

And then the newest witness says
he saw Trayvon hitting
Zimmerman "MMA" style
which is the most inane bullshit
I have ever heard

And it's 11 a.m., my youngest
sister calling and calling, and will
not let me ignore—it's her
first full day of summer vacation
and she's eleven and inside watching
the seismic drag of a murder
trial. I answer:

                              "What."
                    "Are you watching?"
                              "Yes."
                           "Me too."

Silence.

                          "I'm scared."
                             "Why?"
         "I don't think he's gonna go to jail for this."
                         "Me either."
                  "He got mad fat though."
             "Using fat as an insult is dumb."
             "Using dumb as an insult is dumb!"

And then I'm thinking of all circumstances of laughter
we've had to shuck out of ruin, in all these years
Raffi, only as old as some of my favorite books, still
thick enough to lay the plate light with humor, and I'm
thinking of the time she hid the knives, scissors, all things
with edge and I'm thinking about tragedy, how it bleeds

49

through the little mind with keen precision and I'm feeling
the guilt of shortening a child's childhood and it's all
a big arena isn't it, all cyclical and imprecise.

# WHEN I SAY THE HOOD MADE ME, I MEAN:

A sheer violence and a bed embalmed in it, a small girl pretzel legged at the center, soft stones placed at the north and west of her frame, crystals stapled at the southernmost point, the new world a salt capsule, a one-way entrance. Before her nana died there was a brief quiet and then the spirits came and she was besieged with rupture, and talked with them only through series' of bloodlettings,

the blade cold against the stiff brown skin, the dare ripe with noise, so much noise, and is anyone listening (except the pores of these walls) to this girl shrugging out of the mud, sopping with it but limbs activated nevertheless and the stones with a tide of tension below pushing them up up until the spirit exhausts and the crystals fall back into the bowl of the bed, the sugar sticky and stark, a soft voice initiates the beginning of a new life

and then

a hum.

# WILLING IN THE ORISHA

### I.

My body a full echo  I dawdle down to the creek

    Ask the god of blood for
    abundance      continuity

        My offering    the syrup of pressed beans &

a seven-winged tulip

### II.

Later the rains swell the creek with coffee   the storm   a
beckoned sheet
The immortal herself reaping the earth   the tongues cut out of
                    the cows

### III.

I walk in      as the wash    attempts its valiant swallow of
fields
    A cafeteria aid          wipes the cotton from the
counter

    Her bald eyes        aurora with    seeds

       *You brought that*    *didn't you?*

## IV.

valley

My bottom lip a pink venom   My desire a

with legs

Every now & then a troubled thirst
opens my mouth for a song that does not come
I feel it all
until a fixed voice decides

No   *but wait*   *you're the water*

# "BUT THERE WERE TIMES WHEN YOU OFFERED YOUR CONSENT WITH OLDER MEN. YOU CHOSE THEM & YOU WERE NOT AFRAID. WHY NOT?"—FREUD

You don't know the true success of survival 'til you've experienced the adrenaline of a too-close death. What is there to fear when you've licked the edge? It is going to be an oppressively hot summer, the *New York Post* says, but I've got a few of my own stowed away, enough to occupy a foreign desert.

There was one summer, his name was Tito and my sisters still say his name just like that, "Tee-toww" the O a benchmark in the bottom of the jaw. I was just twelve but the gaze itself made me a flame, so no one could tell, I guess,

or no one would tell. He was the kind of heavy swelter that had the whole block at mercy, everyone's connect to whatever they needed, which was much and in bulk. Power is a switch that yokes me up at the waist—I was young & enamored by this pattern of men who shouldn't want me but would risk day to touch the stark chant of me. Each time, I imagined a witchcraft enveloping the bone. I remember,

once, at some low hour in the trough of that summer—my mouth a voyaging boat, Tito's spine a current of illicit knots, his hand a spindle on the back of my coarse head—he looks down at me & moans out "Who the fuck are you?"

I say, and the answer remains the same thereafter[10]:
nobody, who are you?

---

10    *Okay, in any event, Catherine and I were in the pool, swimming and playing.*

# YES, IT IS POSSIBLE

For most of my life I remained unaware of this
the way a wingless arm is unaware of the conceit

of flight, but now I know that, yes, it is possible
to be allergic to a person, it is possible for

the body to be wholly autonomous in how
it chooses to preserve itself, no matter what

fleshy, amorphous image of the heart the synapse
might conjure; a great fire muted by holy water,

a blue room with one pink knob—no matter what
you think you want, it's the body that decides

& will reject whatever antibodies revile its stasis
and in this case, the foreign cell was the Pisces fish—

a twin fish, a two-fish flush, unvirtuous
& writhing in deceit and steeped

in the drama of belonging to too many lies
and yes, I had prayed that he'd finally come

back to me, and that when he'd knock, he'd appear
with one less life, but then he did appear—a xenophile

on a tour of homes—and that would be our last encounter
all I could do was heave at the sight of him

head oscillating dizzily between two different
men, two different lives, so piscean in his

world of elysian highs
but this time my systems nosed down
anatomy buckling out into autopilot
bringing me down to my knees to purge

and it was like this for days: I couldn't stomach
a morsel, my receptors stunted

with the shock of an imminent shift
I wept and cocooned myself into

    a sweat until, at once, it stopped—
    and I woke to find myself at the kitchen table

    perfectly unbothered

    fingering cubes of fresh wet aloe into my mouth
    as if life itself were some benign victory I'd won.[11]

---

11   *Okay dearie, that's it.*

*Hi Camonghne,*

*I remembered something that was a breakthrough for me. I always
kept telling you all that I can't swim, but I also would tell you how my
family taught the young ones how to swim, and that they did it to me
too. So, how did I come to believe that I did not know how to swim?
Well, it happened when I was attacked in the pool when I was eleven
or twelve years old and I was staying with a family in PA for two
weeks as a part of the Fresh Air Fund program for inner-city kids.*

*I was in the pool with Catherine.*

*Now, before I continue, I must say that knowing her name is an
emotional breakthrough for me because up until two weeks ago, I
could not remember my friend's name. Catherine was the daughter
of the family I was staying with but after the pool attack by her male
neighbor, who was about fourteen-years-old, I could not remember
her name. Okay, in any event, Catherine and I were in the pool
swimming and playing. Her neighbor, a fourteen-year-old boy,
of course Caucasian, came in the pool. No one thought anything
untowardly. Then Catherine got stung by a bee. We were looking at
her arm because bee stings don't rise and hurt immediately, and then it
started to swell, get red and she started to cry. We agreed we should go
in the house. She climbed up the ladder and got out the pool first. I was
standing on the ladder watching her go into the house. As I got ready
to go further up the ladder to get out of the pool, the fourteen-year-old
male neighbor grabbed me. He grabbed me and flung me back into the
pool. It's a little fuzzy, but I remember trying to grab the ladder and
he kept pushing me back. Then he grabbed me and we began to fight.
I don't believe I was struggling, I was fighting because now as my
memory returns, I recall that afterwards in the house, when his father
came and beat him, before that though, I remember his face was red. I
did some damage. My brother Dale was proud.*

*In any event, I digress. We fought and somehow, as I don't remember,
I got out the pool. I believe Catherine's father heard the commotion
and came out and that's how I got away from the creep. He was trying*

to pull my bathing suit halter top down. I remember that and that's probably when I went berserk and fought him like a crazy person and I was probably yelling too. In any event, next I remember being in the house and there was the attacker's father, Catherine's father and one or two more white males. And what I gathered by looking at my attacker was that his father and I guess the other males beat the shit out of him. They kept apologizing to me and he was twitching and his face looked bloated and he kept holding himself, so I believe they kicked his ass. These weren't like bad white people, at least that's what I believed when I saw the way he was; he looked like someone that had gotten an ass whipping.

Okay dearie, that's it. I always remembered the story, it's just that I thought I did not know how to swim and it dawned on me that not only did I know how, I used to do underwater tricks and swim from one end of the pool to the other, and used to swim at the beach. So how is it that I came to believe that I did not know how? Well, I surmise that it was the shock of that attempted rape that made me afraid of the water, especially if water got to my neck. He must have tried to hold me and when he couldn't get my underwear off to rape me, he was probably trying to kill me and I fought like hell for my life before Catherine's father heard my screams and came running out. Thank G-d he did. I might have been dead, that young punk would have went to jail, I'm almost certain due to how his family reacted.

So, yeah, I know how to swim, I just have to unlock the fear and the only way is to take swimming all over again. I was almost killed in that water and I've had a fear ever since. How is it that I'm sane? Am I really sane? Okay, time to stop. I had an attack; just thought I couldn't breathe, tears in my eyes. That's all I have to say now. I'm not reviewing for spelling or grammatical errors. You can do that.

Later.

Love,

Mom

# ACKNOWLEDGMENTS

First, the biggest thank you to my mother, who has, almost single-handedly kept me alive—the most impressive feat one could encounter. Thank you for pushing me to want my life, for pushing me to see myself as myself, as more than the total sum of the things that have hurt me. Thank you for being my first fan, my first teacher, and for keeping my lil' ego in check. When I was twelve you told me, "It's not the world's job to understand you, it's your job to understand the world," and I'm pretty sure that statement is what made me choose poetry as the vessel of my understanding.

Thank you to my grandmothers, whose weathered hands and stern eyes kept me soft when the world wanted to make me hard. Thank you to my three little sisters for reminding me every day of the importance of protecting the humanity of the black femme body, for reminding me of the power of being gentle with those you love, for reminding me of the power of being a leader and the power of being led.

Thank you to dad for being one of my best friends, for reading *The Adventures of Brer Rabbit* to me and taking me ice-skating where I discovered what it felt like to fly. Thank you to my stepmom Keisha Gaye-Anderson, the first poet I'd ever met who brought me to my very first poetry reading. Thank you to my little brother Marcus, whose sheer existence brought such joy to my life because I asked God for a brother and then I got one.

Thank you to my aunt Jeanette for being the first cool person I'd ever met and one of the reasons I am the woman I am today. Thank you to my cousins Jazmine, Saidah, Ebony, Diamond,

Deidre, Livi, Shamilah, Shana, and Shamar for being my first friends and loving me even though I forget to call y'all back, and to my uncle Brian who left us too soon but left us with such love. My dad misses his best friend, and I miss the way you smell and your big laugh.

To my synagogue family, thank you for being a safe haven and allowing me to connect to something bigger and more profound than myself.

I almost failed out of high school, but the care and patience of teachers and classmates who chose to invest in the talents I had yet to see in myself got me through. My love and thanks to LGJ High School, to Erik Fogel and Mr. Van Dyke, who introduced me to policy debate and helped spark my interest in the unique complexities of language and the importance of fighting for our ideas.

Thank you to the BCC High School community, to Harold Benjamin who, no matter how much I messed up, would reassure me of my value and my power; to Tashana Williams who spent every lunch break with me during my senior year to teach me about what I wanted to know and for loving me while holding me accountable in ways only a mother or mentor could; to Miss K whose patient teaching introduced me to the world of short stories and sparked my love of creative writing; to Kwame Baird who told me to write my first poem as he awkwardly comforted me through my tears after seeing Malcolm X's murder in the Spike Lee directed film. Thank you to Eric Hogle who introduced me to my love of physics, who helped me realize that the things I thought I wasn't good at were just the things that scared me.

No note of thanks could ever communicate just how thankful I am to Urban Word NYC. I came through your doors as an angry, passionate young woman, and on my first day, walked out with a new lease on hope and potential. I wouldn't be half of the writer I am without the space you provided, the rigor of your curricula, and for blessing us with the safety of community, for introducing me to some of the best friends and teachers I'll ever have. To Aracelis Girmay, whose sweet, sweet lyric inspired my want to be sweet within the rage of my own lyric, who wrote a letter of recommendation when I applied to grad school and couldn't imagine who would vouch for volatile, nineteen-year-old me. To Willie Perdomo, whose Wednesday workshop brought me into Urban Word and kept me there and who came to be my mentor at Cave Canem; he brought everything full circle.

To Michael Cirelli, who built and cultivated spaces unlike any other, whose love for his "kids" taught us to be wary of any teacher who does not love us as their own. To Patricia Smith, Rachel McKibbens, Jeanann Verlee, Eboni Hogan, and all the poetry aunties who helped to usher and protect me in the poetry world. Thank you to Diamond, Thiahera, Lo Anderson, Dom O, Alexis Marie, Jorge, Tia, Kai, Ish, Sean, Jessica Blandon, Tai Brown, Carvens Lissaint, Miles Hodges—that Urban Word hallway holds our memories, our laughter, the essence of our little family, I would be nowhere near the woman I am now without the time we've spent together. Shout-out to dollar pizza, the American Apparel on 23rd and 7th, all the places still holding little pieces of us.

To my squad, my day-ones—Safia Elhillo, Aziza Barnes, Mega—shit has changed, our lives have transformed, and some of us are farther than we are near, but we started this journey together and we are going to finish it together, some way or another. Your friendships, our little family, has kept me hopeful and taught me about true unconditional love. You have fed me, protected me, and charged me. You have taught me, struggled with me through my worst time, and given me some of my best memories. Thanks for the dope birthday parties, for our Sunday family meals, for every poem we've written together, every stage we've graced together, every state we've seen together, every song we've sung together, every fight we've fought. I refuse to leave any of you behind.

And oh, my dear Mahogany L. Browne, my most important mentor, my second mother—thank you for everything. For helping me to find my voice and helping to refine and train it, for showing me that being a Black girl with big fists and a big mouth is a magical blessing, for embodying excellence in every way. Thank you for every push-up, every moment of discipline, for taking the time to raise me. Thank you for every poem you've ever written for me, every door you've opened for me (wooh y'all, I am CRYING) for keeping me safe, for publishing *Yolk* and for making sure I know that I am enough. There is no thank you that could ever truly capture just how important you have been to my craft and my life. Every poem I write is written in your honor.

To my extended literary family, and some of the greatest friends, mentors and aunties I'll ever know: Miguel Algarin, Mary Taibi, Ken Arkind, Chelsea Coreen, Vanessa Hidary, Jamal St. John, Paula Tran, Bambu MC, Lyn and Rich Robinson, Natalie Eilbert, Juliet P. Howard, Jamal, the Nuyorican Poetry Café, NYU Slam, Gia Shakur, Ricardo Maldonado, Itiola Jones, Latasha Diggs, R. Erica Doyle, Lynne Procope, Cookie, Chanda Hsu Prescott, Dominique Christina, Elizabeth Vazquez, Lauren Whitehead, Monica McClure, Laura Marie Marciano, SLAP, Kimberly McCrae, Yahdon Israel, Shauna Barbosa, Michael Lee, Jamaica Osorio, and Adam Faulkner.

All my love and grace to my family and friends at Bard MFA who saw and helped to water the first seeds of this manuscript—Ann Lauchterach, Anselm Berrigan, Maggie Nelson, Rob Fitterman, Renee Gladman, Yasamin Ghiasi, Nora, Layli Long Soldier, Alex Cuff, Daisy Atterbury, Mirene Arsenios, Genji Amino, and to Fred Moten who wrote the blurb for *Yolk*, who taught me that to be a Black poet under the smothering whiteness of the literary world is to be a miracle, who taught me to trust my voice amidst that whiteness, who gave me the references no one else could give me, the references that helped me identify that my work is a study of Blackness, a study of power, who allowed me the academic framework that would inform my entire practice.

To Cave Canem, the home for Black poets. It is truly a home and a haven for our magic, our language, our compulsion toward reimagining and telling the truth. To my Cave Canem family, friends, mentors, my aunties, my uncles, and my cousins—Nicole Sealey, Jacqueline Jones Lamon, Lyrae Van Clief-Stefanon, Evie Shockley, Gregory Pardlo, Cornelius Eady, Rickey Laurentiis, Justin Phillip Reed, Falu, Desiree Bailey, Clint Smith, Natasha Oludakun, Jari Bradley, Tyehimba Jess, Elizabeth Acevedo, Nicholas Nichols, Aja Monet, Dawn Lundy Martin, Tara Betts, Rico Frederick, Taylor Johnson, Tafisha Edwards. Big thank you to Morgan Parker, Nate Marshall, Marwa Helal, and Nick Makoha, Kevin Coval, and the team at Haymarket who have seen renditions of this manuscript across its various stages and have given such love, encouragement, and advice.

To Justin Moore, Kayla Monteiro, Zerlina Maxwell, Latasha Alcindor, Ashley Bernard, Phil, my mentee Egypt, and especially GB Kim who designed this book cover—thank you for being willing ears, for showing up at my little readings with flowers and hugs, for being cheerleaders, and for being some of the best friends I've ever had. I am a better person, a better thinker, and a better artist because of your love.

If you're reading this and see that your name is missing from this inexhaustible list of gratitude, know that without your generosity, your love and your encouragement, this project would just be a collection of pages and a cover. It's your willingness to take this journey with me, over and over again, from cover to cover, that has made this dream come true.

All my love,

Camonghne

# ABOUT HAYMARKET BOOKS

Haymarket Books is a radical, independent, nonprofit book publisher based in Chicago. Our mission is to publish books that contribute to struggles for social and economic justice. We strive to make our books a vibrant and organic part of social movements and the education and development of a critical, engaged, international left.

We take inspiration and courage from our namesakes, the Haymarket martyrs, who gave their lives fighting for a better world. Their 1886 struggle for the eight-hour day—which gave us May Day, the international workers' holiday—reminds workers around the world that ordinary people can organize and struggle for their own liberation. These struggles continue today across the globe—struggles against oppression, exploitation, poverty, and war.

Since our founding in 2001, Haymarket Books has published more than five hundred titles. Radically independent, we seek to drive a wedge into the risk-averse world of corporate book publishing. Our authors include Noam Chomsky, Arundhati Roy, Rebecca Solnit, Angela Y. Davis, Howard Zinn, Amy Goodman, Wallace Shawn, Mike Davis, Winona LaDuke, Ilan Pappé, Richard Wolff, Dave Zirin, Keeanga-Yamahtta Taylor, Nick Turse, Dahr Jamail, David Barsamian, Elizabeth Laird, Amira Hass, Mark Steel, Avi Lewis, Naomi Klein, and Neil Davidson. We are also the trade publishers of the acclaimed Historical Materialism Book Series and of Dispatch Books.